MY MOTHER, BROTHER, AND ME 2024

GLORIA BILLIN

Fans of personal memoirs such as Finding Me and In Pieces by Sally Field will be touched by Bits and Pieces: a moving tribute from a daughter to her mother, and beautiful portrait of three people who loved each other deeply. Whoopi writes, "Not everybody gets to walk this earth with folks who let you be exactly who you are and who give you the confidence to become exactly who you want to be.

Emma Johnson was the key to Caryn Johnson becoming Whoopi Goldberg. Emma cared for her kids, giving them love and advice to help them succeed. Whoopi felt very alone after losing her mom in 2010 and her brother Clyde five years later because they were the only ones who truly understood her.

Emma didn't just want her kids to survive; she wanted them to do well. In her personal memoir, Whoopi shares stories from their life together. They grew up in New York City, going on fun trips and having magical Christmases despite their challenges. Only later did Whoopi realize how tough some of those challenges were for her mom.

MINE

She rises and shines in haziness, twisted on the virus stone floor of the pinnacle. The smell of pee and spoiled straw consuming her noses. Iron sleeves gnawing at the wounds on her wrists. Rapidly she snatches at the retreating dream, wanting to pull it back, to enclose herself up again by its furious satisfaction. However, no, it's past the point of no return. The last ringlets get past her, and she is left in obscurity with her watchmen — three of them inside the phone with her, two out in the corridor.

They are snoozing now, in this faint, desolate hour. Set in the shadows like dolls with their heads fallen forward and their mouths open, wheezing. In any case, soon enough, she knows, they'll be conscious. Before long enough the enormous one, the one they call Berwoit, will smile with his square blue teeth and begin in with his insults. " Lift up your skirts for us, witch. Show us what you got under there. Is it a chicken or is it a pussy?"

Obviously she'll pass on soon. She sees this too in her fantasies. The huge, popping yellow fire in the square, the smiling Diocesan, the horrified, enchanted swarms. The cleric Massieu says it's false. " You're not kidding," he murmurs. Now that she's atoned, she's protected.

Before long, he says, they'll move her to a congregation jail, and there will be no more beatings and no more preliminary, and in the end, the Goddons will disregard her. The conflict will end, and she'll be liberated. " Show restraint, kid," he says. " Give them an opportunity to neglect."

She feels frustrated about Massieu. Knows he's half enamored with her. Indeed, even with her shaved head and the unpleasant burlap dress the Priest makes her wear, even with her ribs extending out like a starved canine's, he takes a gander at her with sparkling eyes, sneaks her pieces of bread and additional cups of water, brings her wormwood ointment for her injuries. She might want to trust him, yet she realizes it isn't accurate. They disdain her to an extreme, the English. They won't be content until they dance on her bones.

Frequently in the evening, when she can't rest, Massieu comes and sits with her. He holds on until the watchmen are wheezing, then, at that point, hauls his low wooden stool over to her cell and sits alongside her in the haziness. Holds the bars with his large pink hands, looks at her. At times he peruses from the Book of scriptures. Different times he sings, jokes, attempts to make her snicker. Sometimes he develops trying, gets clarification on pressing issues: " Is it genuine what they say? Is it true or not that you are a holy person?"

She was twelve whenever she first heard the voices. It was in the nursery in Domrémy, behind her folks' home. A mid year day. Hot and green. An extraordinary breeze moving in the air, the country an uproar of shaking leaves. She was taking bugs out the cucumber plants, gathering them in an old stopped container. Her dad said, "You very much like it since you can stay there and dream," yet it wasn't correct. She loved hunting under the enormous, unpleasant leaves for the dull little scarabs with their dark protective caps and their scratchy snared legs. The peculiar purple and green lights in their protection.

Cockroaches sickened her, however not insects. Bugs appeared to be perfect and some way or another respectable, as minuscule cleaned knights.

As she worked, she considered Catherine, her holy person. Catherine whom her mom told about — the most courageous one of all. She imagined Catherine tall and thin and exceptionally fair, with long weighty brilliant hair and a pale, cryptic spoon-formed face. She cherished Catherine, revered her, yet she was desirous of her as well. Desirous of her marvels. Envious that she had kicked the bucket for her adoration for God. She thought about every one of the Romans that Catherine had instructed to adore God. The Sovereign's a large number of warriors stooping down out of nowhere, bowing their heads in petition, their hearts opened up like shades on the primary warm day of spring. Indeed, even the Sovereign herself bowing, even the Ruler seized by this abrupt love of Christ. She considered how the Head Maxentius had despised Catherine for her power, and of the relative multitude of ways he'd attempted to have her killed: the spiked wooden torment wheel that fell to pieces when the watchmen attempted to attach her to it ... the stream from which she continued to ascend like a plug, regardless of how long they held her under ... the fire that seethed around her yet made no imprint, left her skin cool and white as lilies. Finally they needed to remove Catherine's head with a hatchet to kill her. Jehanne saw the incredible sharp edge blazing, the pale, stunned face turning through air, and she wanted to be just fearless. That unadulterated.

It resembled a fever in her, her adoration for God. Not gentle, not considerate. Consuming. Each night in Domrémy, the ringers rang out in the congregation tower for Compline, and she ran downhill through the wheat fields to be with Him, her feet flying over the grass and soil, her heart beating like a hot red drum. He was the sum total of her thoughts. All she needed.

"Where does God reside?" she'd asked her mom once.

"God lives in Paradise."

"What's Paradise?"

Her mom had looked miserable then. At long last she faced up to the mists and said, "Paradise is God's delightful heaven overhead. Assuming we are awesome, we'll go there to live with Him after we pass on." As her mom talked, her eyes looked so eager that Jehanne's heart ballooned like a sail.

"Might we at any point go there now?"

"No," her mom said. " We can't go there now."

She doesn't have the foggiest idea when it initially flourished inside her, that strive after God. Maybe it was dependably there. She realize that He was the person who made the trees. Also, the breeze in the trees. Furthermore, the unmistakable, cold green stream with the round white stones on the base. Furthermore, the red collect moon. Also, the little dark starlings that plunged and rose above her head at dusk, a great many them rising and shifting and taking off, blazing their dark wings against the flushed pink sky.

She knew this, and the wonderment she felt knowing it — appreciation ascending in her like music, so solid it pushed her to the brink of collapse, made her sob. Please, she would think. How might I much obliged? How might I show you?

Yet, she wasn't pondering it when it worked out. She'd neglected. She was simply sitting in the nursery with her face went up to the sun, paying attention to the breeze shaking the trees, when a voice came unexpectedly, extremely noisy. A man's voice and an incredible spangle of light to one side of her. A glow like daylight on her cheek, down her neck, along her spine. Jehanne, it said. The voice extremely profound, moving through her like thunder. Setting her blood ablaze. Jehanne, my virgin, House keeper of France.

She was unnerved from the get go, sobbing, grasping at the grass as though she expected to be torn away from the earth. Scared and excited. Who are you? she inquired. The light had dazed her. She was unable to see her home.

You know who I'm.

No, I don't.

Indeed, Jehanne, you do.

She knew. In her bones, she knew. It was what she'd appealed to God for. The main thing she'd at any point cared about. Gradually the light started to spread inside her, through her paunch, her hips, her bosoms, her mouth, her thighs, washing through her like daylight, warm and brilliant, topping her off, delivering her ... a bird in flight.

She doesn't have the foggiest idea how long it endured. It seemed like quite a while, yet she doesn't have the foggiest idea. What she knows is that a while later, when the voice and the light were gone, it was horrible. All the world dim and chilly, similar to a burial chamber. Dark trees, dim sky, dark sun. Dark leaves abandoning down the slope. Everything cool, withered, dispossessed. She lay twisted on the ground, crying. Return, please. Return. Needing only to bite the dust, rest. Return.

At the point when she got up, the shadow had passed. Wonder had its spot. She turned over on her back and gazed toward the sky through the riddle of leaves. Everything was increased, humming with life. Singing. The sky totally clear, blue and astonishing. The trees bowing and waving in the breeze. Smell of onion weed and sweet clover in her noses. Cows lowing somewhere far off. Her mom inside, crushing flour, her dad in the field, shouting at the cows.

It's all ideal, all as it should be, she sees. Indeed, even the most awful things. Indeed, even the kid Volo, in his enclosure in Madame de Pois' outbuilding, with his dim cauliflower head and his little skewed eyes. Or on the other hand distraught Lord Charles, running stripped through the castle in Paris, tossing his own poo against the windows. The Goddons and Burgundians roaring through the slopes, setting entire towns ablaze, destroying the ladies and youngsters, taking area, cows, sheep, gold, taking their whole nation free from them. It's all OK at this point. Every last bit of it important, part of His arrangement. Similarly as she, Jehanne, lying in the nursery, is essential for His arrangement, however she knows not how yet, or why. She knows basically that He has pulled back life's shade for a moment and shown her His wonderful fire, illuminated her with His inexplicable fire. Furthermore, she realizes that she will rehash anything to feel that fire.

She didn't tell anybody. She realized they would chuckle, call her insane, a numb-skull, a liar. She kept it inside her, secret, consuming like a little savage sun. Waiting.

There were seven of them in her loved ones. Her mom, her dad, and five youngsters. The three most seasoned were young men: Jacquemin, Jean, and Pierrelot. Quitters, the dad called them. Wastrels. Thus they were. Morose and droop carried, dozing late, kicking the canine. Next came Jehanne's sister, Catherine, the excellence, named after the holy person. Catherine with the dazzling plum mouth and the thick fair cascade of hair. Hair that everybody gazed at in chapel. She, Jehanne, was the most youthful. A spitfire. Dim and careful, with short, tough legs like a jackass.

They lived in the moving green slope nation of northern France, far away from Paris. Far away from everything. Theirs was a place that is known for wide, slow streams and tall old oaks. In summer the fields topped off with poppies, their red upflung skirts gleaming in the sun. In winter their woods was quiet as a congregation.

They were average folks, uneducated, burned by the sun. Their hands and feet were calloused. The new sheep and goats laid down with them inside the house throughout the spring ices, clustered and snuffing in the red shine of the hearth. Jehanne and Catherine folded clothes over their feet to keep warm, held on until summer to wash themselves in the waterway. Be that as it may, they were regarded in their town. Since their dad claimed his property, they were regarded.

They had confidence in one God. They were Christians. Jehanne and her mom and Catherine went to chapel each night for Compline, stooped together on the dull pressed earth floor, their hands tied in supplication. The entire family went on Sunday mornings. Jehanne's mom petitioned God for God's assistance and absolution. Her dad asked God to destroy down the Goddons the way He once destroyed down the Ethiopians. Send them all to Damnation.

They disliked the old woodland divine beings, the agnostic notions. Thought them dishonorable, godless, inept. Jehanne's mom wrapped up her lips and shook her head when their neighbor Mariette hitched herself bare to the furrow every April and hauled it through the sloppy fields on all fours, singing and imploring the old divine beings for a plentiful collect, the fat chimes of her bosoms and gut swinging this way and that, smooth with dark mud. Jehanne's dad didn't hold a mandrake under his bed.

They resided in a stone house close to the stream with four rooms and two little, yet finely made, glass windows. Those windows were her dad's extraordinary enjoyment. " Perceive how fine the mullion work is," he'd tell guests. " Indeed, even Ruler Bourlémont doesn't have better windows."

A glad man, her dad. He considered himself to be a sort of nation lord. He worked energetically, at a run the entire day, furrowing the fields, establishing wheat and rye, taking the cream and hen's eggs to showcase, gathering charges, sorting out individuals for the town watch. The family sat in the front seat at chapel on Sunday. After administrations were done, he circumvented shaking hands, grinning, applauding shoulders. Her dad, Ruler of the Workers.

As a youngster, Jehanne had loved him. On summer evenings, he'd take her alongside him to bring the cows down from the high field close to the old oak woods, the bois chenu. She can recollect his tremendous hand, unpleasant and warm around hers, his long dim shadow venturing out in front of hers out and about. His hand making her safe. At the highest point of the slope, he'd take her to where the little fraises du bois filled in the green and white daylight at the edge of the woods. Little ruby-red berries, cone-formed thus sweet. Intoxicating. They ate small bunches of them as they strolled. At the point when they got done, their palms were wet and tacky, stained red. Her dad held his up and snickered. " Liable," he said. " Liable, blameworthy."

Jehanne didn't have any idea what the word implied then, at that point, however she detected it implied something awful. A virus snake of caution slid through her stomach.

At the point when he started to go distraught, nobody outside the family knew it. He restricted his furies to the house. The red-looked at monster that raised up just once in a while in Jehanne's earliest recollections started to show up to an ever increasing extent, circumnavigating the house with his long teeth uncovered, striking out at anybody who hindered him. " Who do you assume you are?" he would shout at her unexpectedly, for not an obvious explanation. " Who in the world do you assume you are?"

Her mom put it on the conflict. " He hates to see all his persistent effort obliterated," she said, pressing one hand firmly with the other, as though to fend it from taking off. Or then again later she'd say, "This is a direct result of Catherine. He was never similar to this when Catherine was here." Her mom, devout and cherishing, however a defeatist as well, concealing in her requests, her fantasies of Jesus.

They'd been at battle with the English as far back as anybody could recollect. So lengthy that the vast majority of northern France had headed toward the English side. At this point not simply the Goddons to stress over. Presently the Burgundians as well. " Ridiculous swindlers," her dad called them. " Yellow pigs."

Sixty or seventy years, her dad said. For sixty or seventy years the Goddons and Burgundians had been attacking the open country, taking their territory, killing them in their beds as they rested, obliterating their harvests, devouring their knifes. They all had some awareness of the butcher at Agincourt, the horrible attack at Rouen. " Forlorn creatures eating their canines, children sucking at the blue bosoms of their dead moms." In any case, it was only after Jehanne was ten or eleven that the conflict came near her — that she started to comprehend what it implied.

One hot September night she arose to the smell of smoke. Red light was beating on the walls. She sat up in bed and glanced through the window and saw the wheat fields consuming. An ocean of fire. The air dark and rolling, thick with smoke. Their gather annihilated. Her mom sank to the bed, groaning, "Wow." Her dad yelled at her mom to take the youngsters up and conceal in the barn. Then there came an extraordinary roaring of hooves past the house. Uproarious, terrible giggling with it. Her dad ran out the entryway bare with a hatchet, shouting. In any case, the men just snickered at him. Twenty or thirty of them riding a horse, les écorcheurs. Not even troopers that time. No banners or flags, no weaved tunics. Just Goddon hired fighters in old rusted mail, scoundrels braving down of the slopes, destroying the towns and setting them ablaze, taking anything they desired on the grounds that who might stop them? " You going to take us, elderly person? Eh? You and your wilted little prick?" Chuckling as they stacked every last bit of her dad's sheep into a cart and headed out into the evening.

For a period her dad and different men had attempted to safeguard the town. They got together anything that cash they had and went to Master Bourlément, implored him to lease them the old demolished manor on the island in the stream. A major roofless spot with a disintegrating turret, home now just to foxes and a few robins that had settled up in the old homicide openings, the walls streaked white and light green with long cave rock formations of poo. Be that as it may, they were still great, the principal walls, still high and thick and solid. Their arrangement was to conceal the whole town inside during the following attack. " Presently let them attempt to take our domesticated animals," Jehanne's dad said, cleaning his mouth with the rear of his hand.

He and different men started alternating up on the roofs at the edge of the town, standing watch as the night progressed, pacing and slapping their cheeks to remain alert. Be that as it may, in the end it did no decent. They couldn't get the creatures out of their pens and across the waterway to the island quickly enough. At the point when the crooks came through once more, they jogged straight up to the residents who were sliding around on the sloppy riverbanks, attempting to drive the scared calves into the dim water. Blades drawn, giggling, their appearances like cut wooden veils in the torchlight. " Many thanks for your assistance."

After they left, her dad destroyed their home. Heaved everything across the room, seats, tables, bowls, pots, candles, pitchers, plates. Tore the entryway clear off the pivots. Jehanne had never seen him so irate. Her mom remained in the corner, falling down and crying. " Please, Jacques, for the sake of God." Crying until he punched her as well.

Jehanne started to invest more energy in the woodland. It had turned into a wild spot by then, at that point. " The woods returned with the English," her mom said. In their fear, individuals deserted their homesteads, their towns, raced to stow away from the Goddons and live in the forest. They ate roots, grass, here and there their own kids, it was said. They snoozed caves, nestled into the foundations of old trees. Also, the actual forest developed huge, spread out over the fields and old streets and deserted towns, recovering the country. Trees growing up within wore out chapels and houses, creeper plants twisting out of the stacks, leaves winding up high like smoke.

Individuals said the forest were perilous, loaded with starving creatures, wolves and bears, wild pig, yet that didn't terrify Jehanne. She'd seen a wolf once in the street just external her home after a strike. She turned out in the first part of the day and saw her cousin Hemet lying extremely still in a trench. The wolf was lying adjacent to him, smoothly biting on the sparkly pink ropes of his digestive organs. Jehanne gazed, hypnotized by the marvelous variety, thinking, We have those within us? Then her mom ran at the wolf with a digging tool, shouting, "Move away, move away from him!" The wolf just saw her, level yellow eyes like Satan's. Then it returned to eating. No, the forest were better. She preferred it there in the shadows, covered up, quiet. Safe.

Frequently she implored there, in an old tumbled down sanctum to the Virgin Mary she'd tracked down somewhere down in the trees. She'd bow before the wooden sculpture and press her cheek against the sew of the Virgin's robe, kiss her little wooden feet. Help us, she would agree. Kindly assistance us.

She said genuine petitions too in some cases. Supplications her mom had instructed her. " Whenever you are apprehensive, implore God and He will help you," she said. Our Dad, who craftsmanship in Paradise, blessed be thy name ... Thy the hereafter, thy will be finished, on earth for what it's worth in Paradise ...

It astounded her, that request. It resembled a mystery room within her that she could race to at whatever point she needed. Where she could have a real sense of reassurance any time, any hour of the day. All she needed to do was shut her eyes and say the words, and it was right there, wellbeing, the tremendous hand of God on her chest, calming her heart.

Before long she started to implore all over. In chapel, at home, in the fields. Multiple times every day the congregation ringers rang out, and each time she thought, Indeed, presently. Now. She went kneeling down and lifted her face to the sky. She went into the mystery room.

After the day in the nursery, there were three of them who came to her. Three holy people, remaining in the air over her, sparkling. The first harsh, gigantic, kinglike. His hands like prongs. His voice illuminating her bones as though they were candles. He was their chief. She knew when he talked. The profound lion's voice roaring through her, fastening her between her legs, making her need to drop to her knees, to bow her head, call him Sire.

He never needed to say his name. She knew who he was right away. Realized he was Michael, the Lead celestial host. He who is like God. His face topped off the sky. Goodness Ruler, she said, shaking, feeling as though she would fall to pieces with delight. Jehanne, he said. Only single word and it was clear. There's absolutely nothing she wouldn't do for him.

He'd be the one to convey the awful news.

Then came the two virgins. Shining like dandelions. Nurturing, comforting. Holy person Catherine with the miserable spoon face, the hands like cut ivory. Insightful, wonderful Catherine who had broken the spiked torment wheel. Her voice a woodwind of cool water, so clear it caused Jehanne to feel as though she figured out everything on the planet, could include each stone in the lower part of the stream. Furthermore, Holy person Margaret. Full, baldfaced Margaret with the weak earthy colored mustache and rapidly spreading fires bursting in her eyes. Margaret who had battled right out of the stomach of Satan's mythical serpent with her blade. Try not to be apprehensive, cabbage, said Margaret. We'll accompany you as far as possible.

What do you mean, as far as possible?

Nothing, love, said Catherine, embracing her. Set out your concerns and rest now, sweetheart. Rest your head in my arms.

They ridiculed her in the town. Different youngsters. They taunted her for giving offerings to the asking ministers, for taking her choyne bread out to Volo in his enclosure. They said she was devout, an honorable little snob. Whenever they'd attempted to obliterate her. She'd been playing in the field by the Pixies' Tree for certain different young ladies from the town. Hauviette, Mengette, Valerie. They were making poppy wreaths to hang up for the May celebration. It had begun a radiant morning, yet out of nowhere a cloud slid over the sun. An enormous purple cloud, weighty with downpour. Everything developed more obscure, cooler, such as night. The grass looked irate and sharp. Jehanne's heart slithered in reverse in her chest. She strolled a little ways off into the field, to where she figured they couldn't see her any longer, and went kneeling down. She started to supplicate.

At the point when she woke up, they were all waiting around her, gazing down at her. Huge appearances, sneering. Valerie with a devilish search in her eyes. " Take a gander at little Saintie Pie," she said, drawing nearer. " Believe you're terribly arrogant don't you, Saintie Pie?" Jehanne stood up. Her hands had started to perspire. Valerie made another stride nearer. She was taller than Jehanne, maybe a little while more established. A major, solid young lady with a coarse, pale face, enormous bosoms, and little bruised eyes. Odd little stamps like sparrow tracks on her cheeks. Her garments were dependably worn out. Everybody realized her dad was an alcoholic. Everybody realized she'd go into the barn with any kid who inquired. " What's wrong, Saintie Pie, you frightened?" Valerie and different young ladies packed in, with revolting fixed looks on their appearances.

She needed to run then. Or on the other hand breakdown, grovel and ask. " Please, no, don't hurt me." In any case, as she gazed toward the more established young lady, that pale gruff face, she thought, Who is she? For what reason would it be a good idea for her to terrify me? A wild battling soul ascended inside her. " Better than you," she said. " Messy skank." Different young ladies gazed at one another with their mouths open. Everybody with the exception of Valerie. She ventured forward and slapped Jehanne's cheek exceptionally hard. " Little bitch," she said as Jehanne staggered in reverse. " How might you venture to address me like that?"

The world turned into a red, undulating place then, at that point. Everything happening gradually, as though she were submerged, and some way or another likewise exceptionally quick. Jehanne strolled over and smacked the more seasoned young lady directly in the gut. " I do what I need," she said. The more seasoned young lady plunked all the way down, her mouth hanging open, round as an O. Different young ladies burst out giggling. " Jesus!" Valerie cried finally. Then she mixed to her feet and took off.

Later Jehanne strolled down the country road toward the congregation. She was upset for what she'd done. Her sincere weighty, similar to something fastened to the lower part of a well. " Excuse me, Father, I have trespassed," she said as she sat close to Père Guillaume in a faint corner of the congregation. It was in every case somewhat startling in the first place, sitting close to the old minister with his sharp, hard knees and his acrid, stale smelling smell. His dull hands meshed with blue veins. " Let me know your transgressions, Jehanne," he said. She gazed down at the unpleasant wooden seat, followed the grain in the wood with her finger. She considered what she'd done, the startling doughlike non-abrasiveness of Valerie's stomach, Valerie's shocked face as she plunked all the way down. She murmured to the cleric. " I lashed out," she said, her ears hot with disgrace, tears prickling her eyes. Be that as it may, with each word she expressed, she developed lighter, cleaner, the fury spilling out of her, the light pouring in. " God pardons you, my kid," he said finally. " You are pardoned."

Furthermore, the inclination then, at that point! Forgiven. It washed over her like the sea. Wave upon wave. In the end the minister hacked, rearranged his boots against the unpleasant stone floor, and said, "Okay, dear, you can go at this point."

Be that as it may, she would have rather not left the congregation yet, didn't have any desire to leave the inclination. She entered the pale, still nave and represented some time in the extraordinary stone quietness, feeling it on her skin, the coolness, the harmony. She gazed toward her holy people in the stained-glass windows, Holy person Catherine, Holy person Margaret, Holy person Clare ... those tall, miserable, wonderful ladies enlightened by the sun. She thought about their gigantic love for God, their gallant lives, their wonders. How they'd figured out how to be greater, better, to accomplish something useful, battle evil, get away from the mud, the littleness of life. She thought they were the most fortunate individuals on the planet.

She never thought to be enlightening the minister regarding her voices. She realized he would loathe her for it. Wouldn't have the option to help despising her for it. He was a delicate man, Père Guillaume, a good man even, however unfortunate as well. Frightened, shudder underneath his sacred robes. You could see it right in front of him. The dainty purple lips, the dry, papery white hands, the cool, quiet decisions ... She knew whether she told him, he would make sure that she endured. He wouldn't cause the enduring himself, that was not his way, but rather he would let somebody know who might make certain to incur it. " I'm worried about

Jehannette ..." he'd say, and afterward it would be everywhere. They'd beat her until she broke and asked for pardoning, swore it was every one of the an untruth, a dream. Madness. Beat her until she vowed to act, be quiet. Repent.

The main individual she needed to tell was Durand. Her cousin's better half who lived in Burey-le-Petit. Durand of the tall dark boots and the profound breezy snicker. The one Jehanne called Uncle. Consistently at Christmastime they visited him at the large broken house in Burey. He kept a little pet grovel that dozed in a bushel by the hearth and would come straight dependent upon you and press its face against your thighs like a canine. Eat oats right out of your hand. Durand's significant other, Marie, was sharp — a cool, grimacing lady who yelled and slapped your hand in the event that you went briefly cut of meat at dinner — yet Durand was unique. Durand, Jehanne thought, was so kind maybe he had two hearts beating in his chest. At the point when she was a youngster, he was continuously maneuvering her up onto his lap and recounting the holy people. Of Holy person Bernard of Clairvaux who ate just bubbled beech leaves. Furthermore, Holy person Anthony who was tormented by evil presences in the External Mountain close to Pispir. Holy person Anthony who said, "I dread the evil presence something like I dread a fly, and with the indication of the cross I can on the double put him to flight."

Durand adored God as she did: hot and savage. He had voyaged all over France on journeys to visit the sacred spots. He'd seen the Dark Madonna at Le Puy and the brilliant sculpture of

Holy person Foy in Conques. Remained in line practically the entire day to see the jawline bone of the Virgin or a lock of Holy person Peter's hair. The young lady in Rodez who bore the blemish — the injuries of Christ. " They say she was held onto one day by a dream of the execution," he told Jehanne during one of her visits, "and a short time later, openings opened up in her wrists and feet and blood spilled out, as though nails had been passed straight through them. The day I saw her, poor people kid was staying there in the congregation with blood all around her, sobbing and moaning one moment, chuckling madly the following, the entire time with this decent search in her eyes, as though there were individuals in the room that no one but she could see." He took a gander at Jehanne, his eyes sparkling. " It was genuine. I know it. God was there, inside her."

How she'd needed to let him know then, at that point! To pull him right up front and say, "I know. He visits me as well." Yet, she didn't even think about it. Indeed, even with Durand, she didn't even entertain the thought. It was too valuable, too delicate a thing to put out into the world yet. It should have been safeguarded, similar to the rosebush her mom canvassed with feed in the late-winter. It required chance to develop securely, quietly, in obscurity.

From Durand and her mom she had some awareness of the holy people. All the other things she knew about the world came from Claude, the seller. Her dad's companion. When like clockwork he came past that certain point, his enormous cart swaying behind him, heaped high with marvels and garbage — old pots and pots, glass containers, dice, kitchen blades, mirrors, flavors, oils, candles. Whenever he had shown her a coconut as far as possible from Majorca. " Got it off a mariner in Le Havre," he said. A brown furry thing, monstrous as a monkey. He hacked it open with his huge rust-spotted blade and provided Jehanne with a piece of the fresh white tissue inside. A tasty taste. Velvety and sweet, somewhat nutty. She recollects how conveniently it had fallen to pieces in her grasp. " That is the very thing that the islands taste like."

Her dad cherished Claude. After he wrapped up getting out and about in the town, he'd come go through the night at their home. A little, grizzled man, resembling cloves, with large, shining, rich blue eyes that helped

Jehanne to remember the sky in fall. After supper, when she should be sleeping, Claude and her dad would drag their seats up near the hearth and drink until quite a bit later, their profiles glimmering like coin heads in the firelight. Jehanne crawled up into the barn and concealed there in the straw, tuning in.

The Lord's franticness was Claude's number one subject. " Not simply spells any longer; Old Charlie's totally loo now," he said. He told how Charles had gone out into the woodland hunting with his four best knights and killed everything except one of them. Why? " Who can say for sure?" said Claude. It was said that a commotion had surprised him — a twig snapped or a little creature moved in the shrubberies — and unexpectedly he went crazy. Jehanne saw it to her eye, the Lord's wild red face, the Ruler shouting that they were all on a mission to get him. " To kill me and take my crown!" Then, at that point, he drew his blade and hacked away at his men until they lay like broken china dolls on the timberland floor. Every one of the birch trees around them spackled in blood. Every one of the three heads chopped clear off, their frozen eyes gazing at the sky.

"Jesus," her dad said.

"They say he's still wild from it," said the merchant. " Won't let anybody close to him. Tells individuals he's made of glass. On the off chance that anybody contacts him, he'll break like an icicle."

At times Claude talked about the Sovereign as well. Isabeau. The Prostitute Sovereign, he called her. She'd burst into flames with her own kind of frenzy and was going crazy through the realm like a creature in heat. " Opens her legs to anybody who to such an extent as squints at her. The Ruler's dearest companions, his family, anybody she can get her hands on." Claude knew. His sister worked in the royal residence kitchens. She'd watched Isabeau's courteous lady stir up a face cream of crocodile organs, wolf's blood, and pig minds to keep the Sovereign's skin looking youthful. Watched Isabeau's house cleaners carry pails of ass' milk higher up for the imperial shower. " She places belladonna in her eyes around evening time and grins at the unfortunate idiots in the candlelight, allows her hand to brush their roosters under the table." Isabeau's ongoing

#1, Claude said, was the Ruler's sibling, Louis. She'd been seen with her fat white legs secured around his midsection one night in a faint stone flight of stairs, pulling his hair, snorting like a sow.

The entire country, Claude said, was spoiling from within like an old wedding cake. Every one of the aristocrats knew it, however no one would make any meaningful difference either way. They'd either been cleared along into the actual frenzy, feasting on simmered swans and peacocks at their dinners, drinking and wailing into their champagne cups as their nation overturned down around them, screwing each other senseless, or, more than likely they watched from the shadows and plotted to hold onto the crown for themselves. " Louis, Burgundy, Henry, they're all surrounding the privileged position like wolves," Claude said. " Every one of them three screwing Isabeau, every one going ahead, lying there with her out of the loop, stroking her bosoms, and telling her how rich he'll make her in the event that she'll simply persuade poor Charlie to give up the Rule to him."

"My God, she'll destroy us," Jehanne's dad would agree, his face going dull, terrible with disdain. " She'll mean the demise of all."

Jehanne hadn't trusted this from the get go. She thought: It's all so distant. It won't ever come here. In any case, when the strikes on Domrémy started, poor distraught Charles was dead, and Isabeau had done precisely exact thing Claude said she would. Auctions their nation off to the English — wedded her girl to their

Lord, Henry V, and decried her own child, Charles VII, the genuine beneficiary of the lofty position, as ill-conceived, a charlatan. Unsuitable to run the show. Henry became Lord of France, the beast Duke of Burgundy was placed accountable for overseeing Paris, and the Dauphin, Charles VII, had scarcely gotten away with his life. " Presently youthful Charlie conceals in his palace down there in the Loire, poor as a squirrel, terrified of his own shadow," Claude said. " Also, the Goddons win a more area consistently."

The south of France, they knew, was as yet faithful to the crown, yet the English and their Burgundian partners had grabbed up practically all of the northern piece of the country. Jehanne's little town of Domrémy was one of the last pockets in the north that actually waited. In any case, it was clear they couldn't any more. Consistently more towns were singed, more ponies and cows were taken, more towns involved, more laborers butchered in their beds. There was nobody to help them. No law. No sheriff. They were deserted, marooned, obvious objectives for Goddons, Burgundians, criminals.

"Doesn't she see how this is treating the country?" her dad would yell as Jehanne watched from the barn — her jaw hitched, her clench hands grasped tight.

"Does she not mind that the best grape plantations in France are consuming? Every one of the incredible ranches and palaces of Lorraine being plundered, annihilated?"

"Isabeau can scarcely clutch her own chateaux," Claude said. " You think she cares a whole lot about us?"

Once, when they were inebriated, exceptionally late around evening time, Jehanne's dad had gazed upward from where he'd been gazing into the fire, his eyes frantic like a suffocating man's. " Is there no expectation by any means?" he said. " Could it be said that we are ill-fated to become captives of the English, no country by any means, simply 1,000,000 separated lowlifes for them to loot and assault and murder at whatever point they please?"

Claude was reclining in his seat, his long, thin, blue-stockinged legs loosened up before the hearth, the twisted tips of his shoes outlined in the firelight. He took a profound beverage of his wine, then twirled his cup, looking into maybe it held a dream representing things to come. " Indeed, you know the prediction la Gasque d'Avignon made, don't you?"

Her dad fluttered his hand, feigned exacerbation. " Spare me the spouses' stories."

Up in the storehouse, Jehanne inclined in nearer to tune in.

Claude smiled, recounted to the story in a tiresome voice. " France will be demolished by a lady and reestablished by a virgin from the woodlands of Lorraine."

A grunt of chuckling from Jacques. " Not ridiculous likely, given the ones around here."

"You inquired as to whether there was any expectation," said Claude.

"Trust, sure. Not a fantasy."

La Beauty. That was the thing they called Jehanne's more seasoned sister in the town. The Magnificence. She was named after Holy person Catherine, Jehanne's number one holy person, her mom's #1 holy person as well. Her snicker was profound and shimmering and melodic, and her eyes were clear light green, as newly cut cucumbers. The main unbeautiful thing about her was her feet, which were short and bulbous and yellowish in variety, and which she was mindful so as to conceal under her skirt. La Beauty. Catherine La Beauty. " Who am I?" Jehanne would ask her mom. " You're the fearless one," the mother said. " The solid one."

Catherine was the only one their dad won't ever shout at. In any event, when she took a fistful of margarine from the basement and ate it up directly before him, chuckling. He was powerless, looking at her as though he could scarcely accept he'd made something so beautiful. At the point when it down-poured on Sundays, their dad would get her and convey her in his arms as far as possible from chapel back to the house so she wouldn't pamper the sew of her great pink dress in the mud. " Jehanne, run open the entryway for us fast," he'd say. " There's a decent young lady."

Jehanne detested her sister at these times, however it never endured long. It was difficult to remain furious with Catherine. Incomprehensible not to cherish her. Living with Catherine was like living with Durand's grovel.

The room transformed enchanted at whatever point she strolled into it.

The prior night she wedded the city chairman's child, Colin, Catherine and Jehanne had sat up together in their room, talking until quite a bit later. Catherine had brushed every one of the growls and tangles out of Jehanne's unimaginable hair and interlaced it with red silk strips for the following day, her fingers solid and firm, her nails raking delightfully over Jehanne's scalp. At a certain point Jehanne felt so near her sister that she developed strong. " Have you seen it yet?" she inquired. Catherine's eyes flew open. " Jehanne!" she said. However, later she said, "I saw it once briefly." She badly creased her nose. " It was so monstrous." Then she snickered. That wonderful melodic giggle. Profound and murmuring like a child's giggle. " Be that as it may, sort of lovely as well. Like a major blue mushroom."

Jehanne had lain conscious in bed that evening for a really long time, imagining the large blue mushroom and attempting to consider something she could express the following day to make her sister snicker that way once more.

They never realized without a doubt what has been going on with her. Two years after she wedded Colin, she vanished. Jehanne was fourteen when it worked out. Catherine was extremely pregnant. Colin had seen her out by the street, picking daffodils before nightfall. At the point when she didn't come in for dinner, he went searching for her there, however she was no more.

After seven days, Jehanne's sibling, Jean, tracked down Catherine's body under a heap of leaves in the woods. He conveyed it to the extent that the front yard and afterward halted there, frozen, similar to a sculpture. They'd taken her hair — the brilliant cascade — and chopped it off at the scruff. Taken her dress and shoes as well. Pierrelot told her this later, stealthily, for the grown-ups wouldn't allow Jehanne to see her sister's body. " Nothing so that a kid might see," they said. They told her that Catherine had passed on from a hit to the head, yet later, Jehanne heard her dad say it was the disgrace that killed her first. " Disgrace at how the Goddons treated her. Goodness my dear young lady."

That was the finish of him, her dad. He strolled the fields for quite a long time, shouting, crying at the sky. Throwing himself against the trees.

Beating his clench hands against the earth. Later he got back home and set down on his bed. He remained there for a year, gazing at the wall. Jean and Pierrelot assumed control over the cultivating, demonstrated great specialists without the dad there to shout at them. At last Jacques got up. He continued his place in town life, turned out to be old fashioned Jacques d'Arc once more, grinning, gathering charges, applauding shoulders. Be that as it may, at home the cover fell off; he beat Pierrelot for dropping an egg on the floor. Beat Jehanne for giving him a haughty look. Beat her so viciously she was unable to stroll for seven days.

It made the dad visionary, the frenzy. Permitted him to see Jehanne's future in his fantasies. Also, what he saw there shocked him. His youngster, his most youthful, dashing across the fields, wearing a glimmering suit of defensive layer, trailed by a yelling ocean of troopers, her jaw set, her eyes wild, the men roaring and shouting behind her, every one of them riding, running toward war.

He woke in the evening, shouting. Snatched his better half by the throat and squeezed his thumb against her windpipe. " She'll spell the end for us," he panted. " She'll mean the demise of this family." It was past him. His psyche could do nothing with the pictures except for believe that his youngster was ill-fated to run off and turn into a military prostitute, a camp whore, bedding down with any man who might pay. Furthermore, it killed him, its prospect, the destruction of his great family name. His well deserved standing. The possibility that this young lady, this kid, could annihilate his life.

In the wan early morning daylight he concentrated on her, grim and droop carried, eating her bread by the hearth. A little, strong young lady, dull hair, huge bruised eyes, round and wet like a seal's, pink earthy colored cheeks, a country beauty to her. Likewise a rage. An equitable, painstakingly packaged wrath that panicked him.

Afterward, tipsy on wine, he declared that she must be watched. " Watch her or she'll run off the principal opportunity she gets," he said. " Turn into a dirty armed force prostitute." He let her siblings know that assuming they discovered her attempting to run off, they should accept her and suffocate her in the stream. " On the off chance that you don't, I'll do it without anyone else's help, you hear me?" he yelled at her. " By God, you won't disgrace this family. You won't drag our great name through the mud."

Jehanne took a gander at him, her eyes lidded, muddled. " I'm staying put," she said.

Be that as it may, watch her now as she travels through the fair wheat fields behind the little hunchbacked house by the waterway. Watch her walk uphill, this little, expectation figure in an unpleasant red dress, traveling through the fields underneath the late spring sky, a fire, a sort of ownership filling in her eyes as she goes, running her palms over the velvet highest points of the wheat tufts, whistling gently through her teeth. At the temple of the slope stands the high, stirring oak timberland. She moves toward it gradually, with adoration, driving cautiously through the branches into the green house of prayer of leaves, the twigs connecting, pulling at her dress, her meshes, as she moves, got forward through the sun-dappled world until she comes to the old stone raised area somewhere down in the trees.

A little fallen ruin, roofless and spurned. Open to starlight, rainstorms, lightning. The walls are half tumbled down, saplings have grown to a great extent, and toward one side of the space stands the old sculpture of the Virgin, her head shrouded in a hood of green greenery. Yet again jehanne ventures toward the sculpture, strokes the velvet greenery with the chunk of her thumb, takes in the gleaming woodland, then stoops down cautiously before the sculpture, bowing her dim head, talking delicately as she unites her hands in petition. Could it be said that you are here?

She stays this way for quite a while, her eyes shut, her head bowed, pausing. Sporadically she moves her hindquarters marginally or moans, bringing down her shoulders as though a slight change in stance could help her case. A warbler sings out high and clear over her, its tune penetrating the upper vaults of the trees. The old branches lifting gradually and falling in the breeze, their verdant sleeves understandable, miserable as fingers.

Later she lies on her tummy on the woodland floor, palms down, arms broadened like Christ. The cool, nutty aroma of pine in her noses. Could you come? she says. Tears spill from her eyes. The sun sets, a red ball sinking through the trees. The woods becomes faint, cool, and threatening. Still she doesn't move.

"Where could you have been?" says the dad when she comes in hours after the fact, into the evening. The family is assembled around the table, an earthy colored ham shining in the firelight. Next to her dad sits a full, pug-nosed kid who stands when he sees her, smiles like an imbecile.

Jehanne makes a stride in reverse, blood thundering in her ears. Her mom gazes at her. " For the wellbeing of paradise, Jehannette, what's happened to you?" Jehanne peers down. Her feet, her legs, are streaked with mud. A solid stitch of mud ringing the lower part of her dress. " For what reason do you have leaves in your hair?"

She mutters something about nodding off in the fields and hurries to her room. From that point, she hears her mom calling her, yet something holds her back. Maybe her feet are nailed to the floor.

She remains behind the entryway, standing by listening to them talk. Her mom's high, unnatural chuckling. Her dad's constrained, jaunty public voice. After the kid leaves, her dad comes into the room and hits her hard. Her nose starts to drain. An inclination like a blade sticking into her cerebrum. " What in blazes is off with you? Don't you know an admirer when you see one?" He hauls her by the hair into the principal room and tells her mom. " See this little bitch, this girl of yours. Which man could need her for a spouse?"

Outside the moon is full. The extraordinary dark shadow of the beech tree in the yard extends across the room floor and up the wall. " He doesn't mean it," the mother says. The mother sitting on Jehanne's bed, holding her, stroking her hair, clearing the dark outside of blood off of her face with a clammy material. Jehanne lies still, solid as wood. " It's those fantasies he's been having. Those horrendous dreams ..."

Jehanne is quiet. She allows her psyche to meander until she sees the old beech tree in the nursery curve and flex and burst into fire. The tree out of nowhere hot and alive, red and yellow and snapping with fire, venturing a branch into the house, getting through the glass window in the principal room (the cherished window broken!) what's more, getting her dad, hauling him out into the murkiness and holding him tight in those consuming branches until he also bursts into flames, until he also is consuming and shouting, then consuming and quiet, dissolving, disintegrating to a heap of debris on the ground.

She became older. She watched her body start to change. Delicateness where there had been bones and sharp points, hair, a musky smell from the hollows. Misery as well, in the evenings. Torment like a sharp snare, rusting in her heart. Loneliness. Different times delight. Wild taking off bliss. 10,000 birds singing inside her. She strolled through the town in the violet light of day break, swinging her arms, thinking, Thank you, gracious much obliged! Everything moving in her like breeze, shaking her establishments.

It drove her dad wild. Watching his kid change, become strong, clandestine, resistant. As though a wild more bizarre were out of nowhere resting under his own rooftop. An outsider plotting to obliterate his life.

Before long there were rules. Her dad precluded her from heading out into the forest without anyone else. Deny her from the fields, the trees, the slopes. " Not any more running off," he said. " Finish your errands, help your mom, go to chapel, be pleasant to the young fellows when they come calling, that's it in a nutshell."

She needed to ponder the future, her mom said. Marriage. She was sixteen at this point. The time had come. The word made her wiped out to her stomach. She watched different young ladies her age, plaiting blossoms into their hair, squeezing their cheeks, grinning modestly or getting their skirts and moving, flaunting their knees for the young men. Contending over who might live with whom in which dim hut, who might spend their lives furrowing which copied out field, making which dark stew in which miserable hearth, having her hair removed by what man, passing on from which plague or pulsating or pitiful labor ... furthermore, she thought she'd prefer pass on.

She'd prefer be dead.
Listen now, sweetheart. It is the ideal opportunity for you to know your motivation. It was Michael who told her. Michael who came one day while she was bowing among the green shadows in the bois chenu with her eyes shut, face lifted, paying attention to the breeze. It was evening. Unexpectedly the light was there, a

deluge of padded daylight pouring through the trees, the profound Godvoice making the hairs on her arms stand up. You should raise a military and drive the English from France. Take the Dauphin to be delegated lord at Reims. This is God's order.

Her brain dismissed it from the outset. The words drifted through her like submerged sounds, difficult to comprehend. Then, at that point, when she got it, she ran into the trees and hurled, a yellow puddle on the ground.

It was as her dad had imagined. God had shown His desire in the fantasy — her dad simply hadn't perceived. Jehanne said it was unthinkable, what He inquired. Impossible. I'm just a young lady, a worker. I remain unaware of cannons or spears. I have no cash. I couldn't ride a pony. Kindly, ask me whatever else. I'll do anything more!

No.

This is God's central goal, kid. We will help you. God will help you. Go to the Ruler, drive the English out of France. Crown the Lord.

She wailed and ran from the backwoods. " Don't bother me!" she cried. " You ask excessively."
The Congregation of St. Remy sat next to Jehanne's home, not twenty yards away. Isolated simply by a shaggy line of willows and a graveyard of inclining stones featured with light green lichen. The actual congregation, a little peach stone structure with a major wooden cross inside. To her eye Jehanne envisioned Christ extended and incline as a feline

on that cross, his wrists and lower legs jeweled in blood, his miserable, all powerful eyes sparkling from behind the sharp edges of his cheekbones, and seeing him there, she felt less alone. She started investing every last bit of her energy there, misleading her folks, saying she planned to work in the fields however rather crawling back behind the house and into the congregation, supplicating in a seat up close to the raised area.

It was freezing inside the congregation. At any rate, the tips of her fingers went numb, became white and mottled with lavender spots, yet she remained. In the end she disregarded the agony. In some cases there were birds up in the roof, pigeons shuddering and fluttering in the shafts of daylight that poured through the windows. Also, at dusk came the ringers. She sat in the cool wooden seat with her head shifted back, her face lifted to the roof as the extraordinary ringer rang and reverberated through the high stone space, reverberating off the walls, the high curves, the faint, shadowed corners of the nave, the rings of sound undulating however her body, her blood. To her she envisioned an entire universe of chimes, various sizes, ringing inside her. Large weighty ringers in her ribs, her pelvis, her skull, small shrill chimes in her fingertips. Endlessly ringing. Furthermore, that is God as well, she thought. That is you as well.

Up close to the raised area there was a window that was left open all day once summer came. Right external it sat the well that Jehanne's family imparted to the congregation — a dark stony opening that Jehanne had cherished hanging over as a kid, savoring the cool, profound, earth air and the overgrown stone smell, dropping rocks down into the dark sparkling water. Frequently she wanted that she could fall in, endlessly down into the dull unlimited passage, swimming down through the water until she contacted the old heart of the earth.

At some point, while she was asking, Jehanne heard her mom's voice there by the well. There came an unexpected bawl of innocent chuckling. Jehanne got up and strolled to the window. She hunched on one side of it and looked past the leaded corner of the edge. Her mom was remaining in the sun, pulling on the frayed well rope hand over hand and conversing with a kid named Michel Le Buin. The mill operator's child. A fair, pimpled kid with an irate red jawline and slicks of oil on one or the other side of his nose. He strolled around with a glad, haughty look all over, as though he were exceptionally attractive and extremely rich. This goaded Jehanne. Made her long to slap him. " So long since we've had a visit from you," her mom was saying. " I realize Jehannette couldn't want anything more than to see you."

Jehanne moved in an opposite direction from the window, her arms cold. That evening she didn't rest. She lay conscious in her bed, gazing up at the haziness and the faint wood radiates in the roof that seemed like bars upon her future.

A few days after the fact Michel Le Buin came to supper, bowing and perspiring in another green tunic. His hair was spit-brushed across his temple. He held a bunch of vetch under his arm. Jehanne's mom invited

him like a tragically missing child. "
Such wonderful blossoms, Michel!"

He grinned, his ravenous eyes on
Jehanne, sparkling. " They're for
Jehannette."

"How beautiful. Jehannette, put them
in water."

At the point when she sat idle, her dad
kicked her hard under the table.
Talked through his teeth. " Jehanne,
up. Now!"

Gradually she rose. She could feel the
kid's eyes on her as she moved,
investigating her bosoms, her neck.

"A fine young lady she's developed
into," he said.

"Hasn't she," said her dad.

After supper she squatted like a cheat underneath her window, her ears pricked, paying attention to the low laughing voices outside. " Not an ordinary marvel, obviously," her dad said. " In any case, there's power in her. Spine. Beneficial thing in a lady." He was talking like a sales rep, utilizing a similar voice he utilized when he discussed his pigs at market.

"That's what I see. Will she breed?"

Jehanne was gotten by an unexpected vision of herself held up by the lower legs, turning in the air, the men examining her hooves, her rump.

"Oh yes. Did you see the hips on her? She's brought into the world for it."

"Is there not some rudeness in her?"

She could hear her dad grinning in the night air.

"Nothing that can't be remedied," he said.

She ran rapidly through the dew-wet fields in the white fog of first light, up into the forest, endlessly until she figured her lungs would explode, and afterward she halted and concealed herself in the underlying foundations of an extraordinary contorted dark oak. The timberland appeared to be not exactly genuine to her yet, as yet rising up out of the fog, the trees still half covered up, spooky in the cool early light. Jehanne twisted herself up firmly among the underlying foundations of the tree with her eyes shut and her head bowed, pondering, thinking, asking ... What might be the initial step? I can't go straightforwardly to the Lord. He could never see me.

Before long the light started to spread in her bones. Then the low, exciting roar of Michael's voice: Go to Vaucouleurs, minimal one. The lead representative will provide you with a letter of prologue to the Ruler. You will track down allies there.

She needed severely to respond to him. Needed seriously to say, Indeed, I will do as you inquire. Be that as it may, when she attempted to talk, no words emerged. She observed quietly as the light depleted away. Maybe her mouth were loaded up with stones. " Quitter," she said finally, letting the words out. She stood up and cleaned herself off. " Stupid. Moronic defeatist."

Made in United States
Troutdale, OR
05/09/2024

19762932R00046